HELEN BRADLEY

MISS CARTER CAME WITH US

JONATHAN CAPE THIRTY BEDFORD SQUARE LONDON

By the same author

AND MISS CARTER WORE PINK

To Roger, Judith, Claire, Paul, Mark, Stephen and Jean with love from their Grannie

FIRST PUBLISHED 1973
REPRINTED 1973
TEXT AND ILLUSTRATIONS © 1973 BY HELEN BRADLEY

JONATHAN CAPE LTD, 30 BEDFORD SQUARE, LONDON WC1

ISBN 0 224 00891 9

PRINTED AND BOUND IN GREAT BRITAIN
BY JARROLD & SONS LTD, NORWICH

WHEN MOTHER, GEORGE AND I, GRANDMA AND THE AUNTS WENT ACROSS THE SQUARE to St Thomas's Church, Leesfield, on the evening of Christmas Day in the year 1907, we all felt very happy. Grandpa — my Father's Father — had built a nice house at Blackpool with his Farm behind, and all was going well with Father's business. Our little village was a happy, comfortable place to live in, although it wasn't very beautiful; there were too many mills with their tall chimneys pouring out black smoke and soot. We now had an Electric Tramcar to take us into Oldham if we wanted anything special. This was a treat for George and me, and if Grandma wanted something really special, we all went by Tramcar to Manchester, which was a Great Day. We had tea in a café called Smallman's, with waitresses in black, with stiff white aprons, who brought us lots of cakes with icing on. Although they brought us so many, we could only choose one each, in case we got upset, as we had a long journey back on the Tram. Although Manchester was very large, and had such wonderful things to see, it was very tiring, and George and I had great difficulty in keeping awake on our journey home. When we went on a special outing to the Big Shops, we left our two dogs, Gyp and Barney, at home, because Mother was afraid that they might get their paws trodden on in the crowds. They were very glad to see us when we got home.

Mother, Grandma and the Aunts had many nice friends who lived in the Village. There was Miss Carter (who wore Pink), who lived in a rather big double-fronted house. She lived alone, except for her maid Sarah. We thought that Miss Carter didn't like the way Mr Taylor (the Bank Manager) held our Aunt Charlotte's hand sometimes, and the way he looked at her. (Aunt Charlotte was the youngest and prettiest of our Aunts.) Mr Taylor was a widower, and everyone said that it was time he married again. Next door to Miss Carter lived Mrs Maitland and her daughter Emily. Mrs Maitland was very tiresome. She was never sure whether or not she would be well enough to come with us on our daily walk along Spring Lane to the cemetery. But we had to put up with her for the sake of Emily. Emily was so very nice and kind, and Grandma used to say that she would never get out if we did not help her. Poor Emily. She never had pretty dresses like Mother and the Aunts, but she was very nice to George and me, and would sometimes give us a Comfit, or a piece of Tommy Tod Rock to suck, when nobody was looking. Miss Carter, on the other hand, didn't like children. She never looked at George and me, or spoke to us. She never invited us into her house, and would say to Mother, "Jane, I cannot ask you in because of the children." We felt rather sorry for Mother, but she would say with a twinkle in her eye, "Never mind, I've got something she hasn't got," and she would bend down and give us a kiss.

Next door to Grandma lived Mrs Bailey, with her daughter Alice Ann. Alice Ann was very jolly, and a great friend of Aunt Mary. She was getting quite old; Mother said that she had turned forty, which was older than Aunt Mary. The Aunts and Alice Ann went out each Friday to collect the rents from Grandma's tenants, so Mrs Bailey, Mother, George and I would go to Grandma's to keep her company. One Friday night Alice Ann came in, bringing with her a man who was still dressed in his working-clothes, with a red-spotted handkerchief round his neck. He looked very red and uncomfortable as he stood behind Alice Ann, twisting his cloth cap in his hands. Alice Ann took his hand and led him up to her Mother, and said, "Mother, here is Jim Wilson, and we are going to be married three weeks next Saturday." Dear me, it was dreadful. Alice Ann's Mother wept, and said she couldn't understand her, how awful that she should want to marry a man who was only a mill worker — and a widower with four children, at that. Poor man, he went redder than ever, but Mother, who felt very sorry for him, said, "Never mind, I'm sure that everything will turn out all right." Just then, Aunt Mary, Aunt Frances and Miss Carter came in, and Mother took us off home, but not before I saw Aunt Mary go up to Alice Ann and kiss her and say, "Alice Ann, I'm so glad, but are you sure that you can

On a cold February Saturday Alice Ann was married to Jim Wilson and became "Dear Mama" to his four young sons. Alice Ann looked smart in her white serge suit, and Jim Wilson looked ill at ease in a black tailcoat and a tall hat, quite a change from his usual rough working-clothes.

3

manage Jim's four little boys?" Alice Ann laughed and said, "Of course I can, Mary, I can't leave those motherless boys to fend for themselves any longer." I suppose that Mrs Bailey forgave her, for before we knew where we were, Mother was tacking up Alice Ann's wedding dress, and Aunt Frances was doing up her last year's white straw sailor-hat, and putting in a lovely new white feather and new ribbons. Later Alice Ann's Mother agreed to go to live with her, and she found a great deal of happiness in taking care of Jim Wilson's four sons, for she had now become "Grandma", and was very proud of her four Grandsons.

After Christmas, the Aunts and Miss Carter became friendly with Miss Smith. Mother also became interested in Miss Smith's ideas, and took George and me to her meetings. Miss Smith talked on and on about Women's Rights, and women called Suffragettes. We got rather tired of her, but one day she formed her little band of Suffragettes, which included Aunt Mary, Aunt Charlotte, Aunt Frances, Mrs Hope-Ainsworth, John Samuel's wife Florence, and Miss Carter (who wasn't sure what Mr Taylor would think about it). Miss Smith marched them as far as Lees Brook, thinking that she might get other women to join, but some workpeople came along, and the men became very rude and angry, and shouted, "Go home, you women, go home!"

It was Grandma who suggested that we all went over to see Great-Aunt Buckley, and tell her about the dreadful affair. Although it was so early in the year, it had turned very mild, so Great-Aunt Buckley thought it would be a good idea if we all went to Blackpool for a good holiday while the weather was fine. It was much warmer at Blackpool than at Lees. Mother, the Aunts and Miss Carter had planned that they wouldn't bring out their Muslins until May, but they felt a little dowdy in their dark clothes, so out came the Summer dresses, and George and I were soon wearing our white sailor-suits. Mr Taylor couldn't stay at Blackpool for long, but travelled back most weekends, bringing Father with him. Now that the weather was so bright and warm, he also brought Mrs Maitland and Emily. Miss Carter didn't seem to like Emily — I don't know why, because she was so nice and kind to everyone. Even Mr Taylor appeared to like her, and I heard Mother say to Aunt Mary, "Have you seen the way he holds her hand, and how she always blushes Bright Pink." George and I wondered what "blushing" was, and we watched Emily closely to see what she did.

Then one day Grandma received a telegram from Alice Ann saying that her Mother had died suddenly. "Poor Alice Ann," said Grandma, "she will be terribly upset, we must go home straight away." Grandpa was very sorry to hear our sad news, and at once went into our Enchanted Garden to cut large bunches of lilac to take home with us: some to put on our own family graves, and some for Alice Ann. Our little village of Lees was rather cold and bleak, being so close to the Yorkshire Moors, and having so much smoke from the mills, which cut out some of the sunshine. Trees did not grow very well, and it had been a great delight for us to see the beautiful blossom on the cherry, apple, pear and the lilac at Blackpool, all in flower this Spring. When we got home, Grandma told Alice Ann not to worry, as we would take over all arrangements for the funeral tea. What a baking there was! Even Miss Carter helped Aunt Mary to make scores of funeral cakes with caraway seeds and pink icing. There was a roast ham and a tongue, and a large piece of beef. Also three huge sherry trifles and lots of loaves and tea-cakes. And everyone liked ham and pickled walnuts for a funeral tea. As well as all this cooking, we had to get our black clothes out of the chest. Everything had to be tried on and pressed. Then we went across to the Schoolroom to make sure that everything was ready for the Mourners when they returned from the Cemetery.

The day after the funeral was Whit Sunday, so we had our dinner early, and then we all set off to watch the Leesfield Church Whitsuntide Procession, which went right round the village. Then we had to get ready to return to Blackpool, to continue our holiday. How nice it felt to fold away all those

4

At Alice Ann's Mother's funeral Mother bade me put on my black hat and run home with my go-cart for more butter. Only the day before it had been my beautiful white straw hat, but Aunt Frances had dyed it for the funeral, and oh dear, it had become so tight that my head wouldn't fit inside it! George, who came with me, said, "I see water coming out of your eyes …".

Every morning a girl carrying a beautiful doll walked along the sands with her governess. Oh, how I hoped that some day she would stop and let me hold her doll! Once she held it up so that I could see it, but the governess wouldn't allow her to speak to me.

heavy black clothes, and put them back in the chest. How lovely to get out our Summer dresses again. Back again at dear old Blackpool, the sun shone, the sky was blue, and the golden sands were clean and lovely. Grandpa had taught us to love gardens, so George and I made lots and lots of lovely gardens on the sands – with shells for flowers, and bits of driftwood for trees. The time passed very happily for us, but I heard Mother and the Aunts discussing Miss Carter, Mr Taylor and Dear Emily. Miss Carter wasn't always happy, and she went very quiet over such a small thing as Mr Taylor holding Dear Emily's hand.

It was much quieter in Blackpool now. A lot of workpeople never went on holiday, but they came to Blackpool for the day, on Sunday School outings, or on other Day Trips. There were also the Wakes Weeks. A Wakes Week is a town's annual holiday, and the Lancashire and Yorkshire towns staggered their weeks' holidays to help the boarding houses to cope. The more fortunate families would come to Blackpool for a week. Those who were well-to-do might stay longer. Soon it would be Oldham and Lees Wakes and Father and Mr Taylor and lots of friends from Lees would come. As soon as Father and Mr Taylor arrived, Grandpa planned a trip on the *King Orry*, which sailed from Fleetwood to the Isle of Man. When we arrived, Grandpa, who loved ships, took us to see a three-masted schooner which had just arrived from Russia with timber for the Island. We watched the sailors, dressed in quaint clothes, furling the sails. She was a fine ship; not large, but built to stand up to the heavy North Seas. Grandpa said that she had sailed close to the Arctic Circle.

The days were beginning to close in a little, and on a beautiful September day we went in the wagonette, drawn by Prince, our large black horse, to the farm at St Michael's. We went to buy barrels of apples to go back with us in the Luggage Van, when we went back to Lees. These were our Winter store of fruit. Then Mr Taylor arrived at Blackpool to escort the ladies back to Lees, for Mother, the Aunts, Miss Carter and Grandma were going, leaving George and me and the two dogs, Gyp and Barney, at Blackpool for another few weeks. When they had all gone, George and I felt rather lonely, but Father's Cousin Alice came to look after us. She let us help her tidy up the Enchanted Garden, and we had a fire to burn up all the rubbish. Also we collected a great deal of kindling wood for Grandpa to light his fires with during the Winter. One evening George and I were alone in the Enchanted Garden. I did not like to feel afraid, but George thought he could hear an animal breathing, and he thought it might be Biddy Murphy's Tiger. Biddy Murphy (who had lots of children) lived opposite the Murgatroyds, and she used to tell us about her Tiger, which, she said, she had brought from "Owd Ireland". He was always about somewhere, and if children were naughty, and didn't behave themselves, she had only to call "Tiger, Tiger", and he would soon have those children for his dinner. George imagined the Tiger might have come to Blackpool in the Luggage Van.

Now that it was November, the days were growing cold, and the day before Father came to take us home, it snowed. We felt rather sad at leaving, but when we finally got home into our big warm kitchen, with Mother there so glad to see us, how happy we were! On the following day, Grandma came, with the Aunts and Miss Carter, to talk about Christmas, and there were little whisperings about the presents they were making. Two days before Christmas, everyone came to help with the Baking. Extra bread and tea-cakes had to be baked, and lots of mince-pies. There was also plenty of apple sauce and stuffing to be got ready. How good our kitchen smelt, and how warm and comfortable! On Christmas Eve the moon shone bright and clear and the snow lay Crisp and Even, and out in the night we sang our carols: "Oh, Come, all Ye Faithful", and the lovely old Carol "While Shepherds Watched their Flocks by Night". And the white frost glistened on the trees so that the valley was filled with Light, and Hope, and above all, Love, which came down at Christmas. Soon the peaceful, happy year was to end, the year 1908.

ON THE evening of Christmas Day, the bells rang out merrily as we all, except Mrs Maitland and Dear Emily, set out for church. Mrs Maitland said she didn't feel very well, and would rest a while, and would perhaps feel better by the time we all arrived home. We were looking forward to singing the carols and meeting Mr Taylor (the Bank Manager), who was coming back to Grandma's with us. We were going to light the tree and have crackers and games and a good supper.

"GET YOURSELF off home!" shouted the men when they saw Miss Smith and her little band of Suffragettes, who had marched out on a cold January day. It was rather frightening. One man shook Miss Carter (who wore Pink) and she fainted in the middle of the road. Father came home with the news that some dreadful women had been walking through the streets shouting "Votes for Women". "Fancy women wanting the vote—never heard of such tomfoolery," he said. "Jane, I hope that neither you nor your sisters have anything to do with it." Mother said, "No, Frederick, of course not," but she looked at George and me with a twinkle in her eye.

W E TOOK a short cut across Glodwick to Great-Aunt Buckley's, and met Mr Taylor, who
was walking with Mrs Maitland and Dear Emily. Mother and the Aunts wondered how
he had met them so early in the afternoon. When he saw Miss Carter he was most attentive,
and held her hand and hoped she was feeling better after fainting at the Suffragette Meeting. She said
she was still rather weak and her heart still fluttered. "Umph," said Aunt Mary, who didn't care much
for Miss Carter, but only George and I heard her.

GREAT-AUNT BUCKLEY thought that we ought to go to Blackpool early, instead of waiting until after Whitsuntide, especially after Miss Carter's dreadful upset. Mother also was still feeling shaky after that common man had shouted at her, and poor Aunt Mary said a woman had pulled her hat over her eyes and her hat pins had very nearly scalped her. So we went to Oldham to look at Buckley & Proctor's shop, to buy what we needed for the holiday. Miss Carter went in a Hansom Cab, but she felt better after seeing all the lovely materials and clothes, and she returned with us on the Tram.

ONDAY was the Great Wash Day in preparation for going to Blackpool. Sarah came at six o'clock to light the boiler fire, which was in the wood shed. Although it was only the end of March, all the frilly petticoats and Summer muslins had to be got ready for packing in the big trunks, and ready for the railway lorry to take them to Mumps Station. What a day it was! Even Miss Carter helped by bringing some of her special clothes to go in our new Washing-Machine, which Father was very proud of, but Mother, the Aunts and Sarah found very hard work. What a pile of ironing, airing and folding there was! Grandma made a huge pan of potato hash and a lot of apple fritters.

IT WAS our last walk along Spring Lane before setting off for Blackpool the next morning. Grandma, the Aunts and Miss Carter called for us, and as we walked along, talking about all the little things which had to be done before the cabs came to pick us up the following morning, Willie and Annie Murgatroyd came running up to George and me. Annie said that they would see us at the Station in the morning, as they were going to their Aunt's at Blackpool. "What's the matter with Willie?" asked Grandma. "He's got the mumps," shouted Annie. "Oh, dear me," said Mother, "that's the last straw. Put your hankies up to your noses, children, in case he has left any germs behind." "I've never had mumps," said Miss Carter. "Look, Mr Taylor is coming, let us all go back quickly."

GRANDPA was waiting for us on the platform at Waterloo Road Station. Mother hurried George and me and the dogs (Gyp and Barney) and Miss Carter and Mr Taylor quickly up the steps and into Grandpa's wagonette, because Willie and Annie Murgatroyd came running after us. Grandpa stopped Willie, and told Annie to take him back to his Mother. Annie said it didn't matter really, he'd only got the mumps and was very cross, and as we hurried along we could hear him screaming and roaring. We had to leave Father, Grandpa and the three Aunts to attend to our luggage and our two cats, Martha and Nelson, who had come with us.

"OH, THE tide is in." George and I had so looked forward to playing on the sands on our first day at Blackpool, but we couldn't because of the tide. "Never mind," said Mother, "we'll go on the Pier and see if Fred Walmsley's Pierrots are there." They were just beginning their Show with a new song.

> "In the year nineteen hundred and nine,
>   We shall all have a jolly fine time,
>   For the world, you see, will belong to me,
>   In the year nineteen hundred and nine."

How I glowed! How I felt that something wonderful was going to happen! With a feeling of great joy, I ate one of Pye's ices, while Mother, Grandma and the Aunts drank Sandow's Cocoa.

IT WAS a beautiful April evening, and too early for George and me to go to bed, so Mother said, "Don't let us stay indoors, let us go into the Enchanted Garden, and look at the wild cherry blossom, it will soon be over." So we put on our hats, and the Aunts and Miss Carter collected their scissors to cut bunches of sweet-scented narcissus flowers to take back to their lodgings. Mr Taylor and Father had gone out for the evening, and Miss Carter gathered an extra bunch to give to Mr Taylor's landlady, so that she would be extra kind to him.

GRANDPA had to see a Farmer at Fell Foot. He asked us to go with him, knowing how much George and I would enjoy the train journey to Lakeside. He knew also that we would enjoy being rowed across Lake Windermere. He said that we would see lots of big mountains. But, alas, when we got there everything was wrapped in a soft mist. It was most disappointing, especially as we had left Blackpool in all the glory of a May morning. However, we ate our picnic lunch and picked pretty little wild daffodils. Mother, the Aunts and Miss Carter were beginning to feel anxious because some cows were coming into our field. We were glad to see Grandpa, and to hurry into our boat out of their way.

15

IT WAS a fine morning, so Grandpa said, "Let us all go to Rawcliffe Hall," which was not far away. So away we went in the wagonette, with Prince, our black horse, clip-clopping through the lanes to the Park. Grandpa went to see a Farmer friend of his about some cattle, so while they talked, Mother, the Aunts, George and I and Gyp and Barney walked through the lovely Park. We left Miss Carter and Mr Taylor deep in conversation, but when Aunt Charlotte looked back, she saw Miss Carter hurrying towards us and Mr Taylor was walking behind. "Oh!" said Mother to Aunt Mary, "Now what has happened, she's in a dreadful huff."

IT WAS Whitsuntide, and this year we had intended staying on at Blackpool a little longer, but Grandma received a Telegram saying that Alice Ann's Mother had died. Grandma said that we must go home right away and do all we could for poor Alice Ann. There would be a lot of cooking to do for the funeral tea, and Alice Ann would be too upset to cope with it herself. So we got Sarah to come and help, and on the day of the funeral we had everything ready in the Schoolroom. But when Mother looked up and saw that nearly all the villagers were coming, she said, "Oh, dear me! I'm sure that we shall not have enough ham to go round all those people." But we managed very well.

THE DAY after Alice Ann's Mother's funeral was Whit Sunday. We all started out early to watch the Leesfield Church Whitsuntide Procession. It was a lovely day, and we saw the Hope-Ainsworths looking very smart. Mrs Hope-Ainsworth was wearing a dress of the latest colour — Parma Violet. John Henry, with his wife and four children, walked behind them. George and I saw Willie Murgatroyd, who scowled at us.

GEORGE and I would have liked to walk behind the Band, but Mother said it wasn't seemly while we were wearing Black for Alice Ann's Mother; so we all stood and watched as the Whit Walk made its way up the High Street. I didn't like my "Black", and was wondering what I was going to do about getting a new straw hat. Aunt Frances had dyed my nice white hat with a dreadful Black Dye out of a bottle, and the smell—and oh! the awful stiffness of my lovely hat! That night Mother and the Aunts folded away their mourning clothes, for tomorrow we were going back to Blackpool to continue our holiday.

WHEN we arrived at Victoria Station, Manchester, on our way back to Blackpool, Father suddenly remembered that the King and Queen were driving through the City. He said that if we went down by the Cathedral we would have a good chance of seeing them. Just as we got there we could hear people cheering, and along came the King and Queen in an open landau, accompanied by Lord Derby. "Now be ready", said Grandma, "to curtsey; and you, George, must salute." I curtsied quite low, because Grandma said that the Queen had brought much happiness, good taste and new ideas into our lives. I tried not to stare, but I took one peep at the Queen and I was sure that she had a dear little gold crown on top of her hat, which was made of violets. When I told Mother she said, "Nonsense, child, she wouldn't bring her gold crown to Manchester," but I shall always think of her as wearing her gold crown.

WHEN the weather was rough at Blackpool we took our afternoon walk along the Green at Lytham, accompanied by Miss Carter, Mrs Maitland and Emily. Willie and Annie Murgatroyd came also, because they wanted to fly their kites; they were rather mean, and wouldn't allow George or me to hold them. Soon we saw Mr Taylor coming along to take us home, but as soon as he saw Emily he took both her hands and they just stared at each other. Miss Carter didn't like him going straight to Emily. Neither did Mrs Maitland, Emily's Mother, who made a fuss and said she felt ill, and we had to go back quickly.

"JANE, you must get the children home," said Mr Taylor to our Mother, "I'm sure that we are in for a storm, just look at that cloud." And it was such a lovely sunny morning, and George and I had been looking forward to a walk on the sands. When Mr Taylor insisted that we turn back, Miss Carter looked very cross and walked on a little way, but when she saw Mr Taylor walk beside Dear Emily, she soon hurried back to join us. Mother said afterwards that Mr Taylor was a nuisance — he was afraid of rain if he hadn't his umbrella with him. It didn't rain after all — the cloud soon went away and the sun shone again.

22

"GOOD gracious," said Mother, "if those children aren't on the donkeys again!" But the Donkey-Man, whose name was Tom, was just letting us sit on their backs while everybody had stopped to have a chat with Mr Taylor. It was growing dusk and the tide was coming in, and Mother, the Aunts and Miss Carter thought it very kind of Mr Taylor to come to escort us home. Emily Maitland was just behind him, and as he turned, he took her hand, and Aunt Frances told Mother afterwards that she was sure that he said "My Dear", but whatever it was that he said, Emily went Bright Pink. Miss Carter looked hurt, and never spoke a word all the way home.

ON FRIDAY mornings we usually went to Fleetwood with Grandpa to get some fish, but on this particular morning he said, "What about us all going for a sail to the Isle of Man." The day was fine and warm, the sea was calm and very blue, and we would reach the Island in time to call on Cousin Annie Sugden and have dinner with her. So Mother, George and I and the Aunts set off, while Grandpa and Father went to bring Miss Carter and Mr Taylor, Mrs Maitland and Dear Emily. We were glad when they arrived, so that we could all go aboard the *King Orry*, a very fine but noisy paddle-steamer. We enjoyed our sail, and also our dinner with Cousin Annie Sugden, where we had our great favourite—Groudle Pudding, a delicious sponge with marmalade mixed in.

WE SEARCHED for the first of the blackberries along the path by the River at St Michael's, near Blackpool. It was a warm September evening, and everyone had enjoyed a good tea at the Farm. George and I had gathered fresh eggs for tea, and there was home-cured ham, and now we were waiting for Grandpa to finish his talk with the Farmer, and bring Prince and the wagonette to drive us home through the pretty lanes, with the sweet scents of the hedgerows.

THE LAST day of the holidays was rather sad. Everyone was going home tomorrow except George and me. Aunt Mary, who was always ready for an outing, suggested that we all took baskets and went to our little wood to gather blackberries to take home. Mr Taylor came with us to help carry them back. Miss Carter was much kinder than she had been when Mrs Maitland and Dear Emily had been with us. I heard Mother and Aunt Frances whispering that they had expected Mr Taylor to propose this Summer, but he hadn't done so. "And", said Mother, "just look how he has been holding Dear Emily's hand. And that day when we all went to Lytham, I'm sure that I heard him say 'Dearest'."

26

THE NEW Moon was in the sky, and the mists of November were beginning to creep into our Enchanted Garden. One evening, George and I stayed behind after Cousin Alice had gone home, to watch the fire burn down. It got very quiet and lonely, and George thought he could hear an animal breathing; he thought it might be Biddy Murphy's Tiger. Then I wished that Cousin Alice would come back, and we called out, "Cousin Alice!" To our great relief, there she was, coming back for us. We told her about Biddy Murphy's Tiger, but Alice just laughed and said that there were no Tigers in Grandpa's Garden, nor in Lees either.

"COME, children, we must give the birds their dinner," said Alice. It would be the last look at the Enchanted Garden, for George and I were going home, so it was with a mixture of sadness and pleasure that we said Goodbye to the birds, the trees, and all the secret things that lived there. We told the birds that we would see them again in the Spring, and we were sure that they would understand that we had to go home to get ready for Christmas. And when we thought of Christmas, we were so very glad.

A WEEK before Christmas, the Aunts required cottons and silks to finish off their Christmas Gifts. Although it was just starting to snow, we set off for the Needles and Pins Shop at Rhodes Bank in Oldham. Just as we were crossing Yorkshire Street, a lot of bulls came out of a side street, and Grandma, Mother, George and I, and the dogs Gyp and Barney ran and jumped on the front of a Tram. The driver was very kind, and allowed us to stay on the Tram until all the bulls had been driven away. Miss Carter and the Aunts dashed madly down into the Women's Conveniences, while Mr Taylor was very brave — he wanted to see that we were all safe before running out of the way himself. After the fright, Grandma said that we had better all go into Bullough's Café and have a cup of tea.

"JANE, do you think that Mr Taylor will call?" said Miss Carter (who wore Pink). She was looking anxiously at Mother, who was just about to say, "I hope not," when there was a knock at the door, and Mr Taylor (the Bank Manager) walked into the kitchen. He was really quite nice about being shown into the kitchen, and ate a mince-pie, but would not stay for a cup of tea. He thought it better that he should see Miss Carter home as the weather was looking doubtful. Mother and Aunt Mary were busy with the Christmas Baking, and the Aunts were making secret presents. To think that there were only a few more days left to Christmas!

CHRISTMAS Eve was bright and clear, so Mother said that George and I could go with the Aunts, Miss Carter, Mr Taylor, Mrs Maitland and Dear Emily to join the Carol Singers down Milking Green. We were just in time to sing "Christians Awake", which everyone sang lustily. We ended with "Let there be Light". The fields and trees were shining white in the light of the Moon, and there *was* light, for Love came down at Christmas, and the year 1908 had almost ended.